This Notebook Belongs To

____

www.ingramcontent.com/pod-product-compliance
Lightning Source LLC
LaVergne TN
LVHW060209080526
838202LV00052B/4220